WHAT IS A
REFUGEE?

ELISE GRAVEL

schwartz & wade books • New York

A refugee is a person,
just like you and me.

Refugees had to flee their country because they were in danger.

Some of them had to flee because their country was at war.

Some had to leave because powerful people didn't like what they thought or said and wanted to hurt them.

Others had to leave because people didn't accept their religion, or hated them because they were different.

Most refugees would have preferred to stay in their country with their friends and family.

But it was too dangerous. Also, often, their homes were destroyed and they didn't have anything left.

Refugees had to find another country to live in, and that's not easy.

There are countries that don't want to welcome more refugees.

While they were waiting for a new country to welcome them, many refugees had to stay in camps, where life was hard.

Refugees were lucky if they could find a country where they could live a normal life and do normal things like:

Go to school and make friends.

Work.

Live in peace and safety.

Just like you and me.

REFUGEE KIDS SPEAK

I met some refugee kids while writing this book and asked them to tell me a bit about themselves. Here is what they had to say:

"My name is Ayla. I had to leave Syria because of the war. I love to draw with my sister. We make funny comic books."

"I'm Majid. I come from Sudan. There was a lot of fighting. I'm very good at soccer. I could play all day."

"My name is Roseline. My family is from Haiti. My grandmother and two of my cousins couldn't come with us. I miss them so much!"

"My name is Musa. I come from Afghanistan. I love video games, especially Fortnite. My parents think I play too much."

"My name is Nala, and I left Somalia because there was a war and a drought. What I love about my new country is Halloween. We didn't have that where I come from."

"My name is Sebastian, and I used to live in Cuba. We can't live there anymore because my parents don't agree with the government. I want to be a veterinarian when I grow up because I love animals."

SOME FAMOUS REFUGEES

MADELEINE ALBRIGHT's family first left Czechoslovakia in 1939 to escape the Nazis. In 1948, when Madeleine was eleven, she and her family fled Czechoslovakia once more, this time for the United States, when communists took over her country. At the age of sixty, she became the first woman to be appointed Secretary of State.

BOB MARLEY, the reggae superstar, had to flee his beloved Jamaica when people who didn't like his political ideas tried to kill him in 1976. He recovered in the Bahamas and then moved to England, where he recorded more reggae hits.

Born in Pakistan, MALALA YOUSAFZAI fought for Pakistani girls to have the right to go to school. When she was fifteen, she was shot by someone who didn't like what she stood for. She escaped to England, where she continues to champion girls' rights to an education and was awarded a Nobel Peace Prize in 2014.

ALBERT EINSTEIN left Nazi Germany in 1932 when Jews like him were being persecuted, and he found refuge in the United States. His theories about light, matter, gravity, space, and time have completely changed the way we understand the universe.

When she was a child, ANNE FRANK and her family fled Germany for the Netherlands to escape the Nazis. They hid behind bookshelves at the top of a building for two years, but they were eventually found. Though Anne died in a concentration camp, the diary she kept lives on and has been published around the world.

LUOL DENG and his family had to leave South Sudan when he was five years old and a civil war broke out. At fourteen, he came to the United States, where he became an all-star in the NBA!

FREDDIE MERCURY's family fled Zanzibar for England to escape a violent revolution in 1964, when he was a teenager. He became a rock star, and his band Queen still makes people dance and sing.

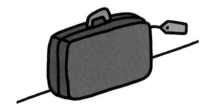

Text and illustrations copyright © 2019 by Elise Gravel
All rights reserved. Published in the United States by Schwartz & Wade Books,
an imprint of Random House Children's Books, a division of Penguin Random House LLC, New York.
Schwartz & Wade Books and the colophon are trademarks of Penguin Random House LLC.
Visit us on the Web! rhcbooks.com
Educators and librarians, for a variety of teaching tools, visit us at RHTeachersLibrarians.com

Library of Congress Cataloging-in-Publication Data is available upon request.
ISBN 978-0-593-12005-7 (hardcover)
ISBN 978-0-593-12006-4 (lib. bdg.)
ISBN 978-0-593-12007-1 (ebook)

The text of this book is set in Grosse Molle.
The illustrations were rendered digitally.
Book design by Rachael Cole

MANUFACTURED IN CHINA
1 3 5 7 9 10 8 6 4 2
First Edition